Little
BOOK
of SAINTS

Volume 3

Written by
Susan Helen Wallace, FSP
Illustrated by
Tom Kinarney

BOOKS & MEDIA
Boston

Library of Congress Cataloging-in-Publication Data

Wallace, Susan Helen.
  Little book of saints / written by Susan Helen Wallace ; illustrated by Tom Kinarney.
      p. cm.
   ISBN 0-8198-4526-4 (pbk.)
 1. Christian saints--Biography--Juvenile literature. I. Kinarney, Tom. II. Title.

   BX4658.M75 2005
   282'.092'2--dc22
                                              2004019192

All rights reserved. No part of this book may be reproduced or transmitted in any form or by any means, electronic or mechanical, including photocopying, recording, or by any information storage and retrieval system without permission in writing from the publisher.

"P" and PAULINE are registered trademarks of the Daughters of St. Paul.

Copyright © 2009, Daughters of St. Paul

Published by Pauline Books & Media, 50 Saint Pauls Avenue, Boston, MA 02130-3491

Printed in U.S.A.

www.pauline.org

Pauline Books & Media is the publishing house of the Daughters of St. Paul, an international congregation of women religious serving the Church with the communications media.

1 2 3 4 5 6 7 8 9   13 12 11 10 09

In this book you'll meet eleven saints and blesseds. Saints and blesseds are good friends of God, and they're our friends, too. We can ask them to help us become more like Jesus, the Son of God. We can ask them to pray for us and with us.

Have fun learning about these new friends!

Contents

Saint Peter Claver	4
Saint Brigid of Ireland	6
Saint Damien of Molokai	8
Saint Elizabeth of Hungary	10
Saint Dominic Savio	12
Saints Ann and Joachim	14
Saint Paul Miki	16
Blessed Kateri Tekakwitha	18
Saint Alberto Hurtado Cruchaga	20
Blessed Teresa of Calcutta	22

Saint Peter Claver

Peter lived in Spain. When he was twenty-two, he became a Jesuit priest. His friend Brother Alphonsus told him about some Africans. Many were being kidnapped. Slave ships took them far away to the New World. Father Peter had to help them! He sailed to Colombia. There he found many frightened, sick Africans. Father Peter served the enslaved people for forty years. He believed that everyone should be treated kindly and with justice. Father Peter baptized many of the Africans. He taught them to love Jesus.

Saint Peter, you helped many suffering people. Teach me to be kind to everyone, too.

> Saint Peter lived from 1580–1654.
>
> He was born in Spain.
>
> We celebrate his feast day on September 9.

Saint Brigid of Ireland

Brigid's parents were baptized by Saint Patrick himself. As a child, Brigid was kind and good. One day she gave a pail of milk to a poor family. She prayed that her mother would not be upset. When she got home, her pail was full again! Brigid wanted to follow Jesus. She had seven good friends. With them, she started the first convent in Ireland. Soon the convent became a center for religion and art. She started other convents, too. Brigid died many years later. She was buried near Saint Patrick.

Saint Brigid, help me to spread Jesus' love as you did.

Saint Brigid lived from around 450–525.

She was born in Ireland.

We celebrate her feast day on February 1.

Saint Damien of Molokai

Joseph got in lots of trouble when he was young. But when he grew up, he changed. He became a priest known as Father Damien. He went to Hawaii and worked hard to spread the love of Jesus. He heard about some people who were very sick with leprosy. They lived on an island called Molokai. Father Damien took care of them. He built houses and brought in clean water. After fifteen years, he caught leprosy too. Father Damien helped over a thousand sick people on Molokai.

Saint Damien, please show me how to be helpful to my family and friends.

Saint Damien lived from 1840–1889.

He was born in Belgium.

We celebrate his feast day on May 10.

Saint Elizabeth of Hungary

Elizabeth was a princess. She married Ludwig, who was a king. They had three children. One winter, Ludwig died. His relatives sent Elizabeth and her children away from the castle. Some Franciscan brothers helped them. Elizabeth's family helped them, too. After that, Elizabeth understood what it was like to be poor. Soon Elizabeth wanted to help others who were poor. She built a hospital. She started a shelter. She cooked meals for homeless people. Elizabeth worked hard to make the world a better place.

Saint Elizabeth, please help me to be cheerful in good times and in bad.

Saint Elizabeth lived from 1207–1231.

She was born in Hungary.

We celebrate her feast day on November 17.

Saint Dominic Savio

Dominic was a blacksmith's son. He had a big dream. He wanted to become a priest. He had lots of friends at school and always studied hard. Often he visited the chapel to pray to his "best friend," Jesus. Dominic wanted to be like his school principal, Father John Bosco. When Dominic was fourteen, he became very ill. He went home to recover, but he didn't get better. Soon he joined Jesus in heaven. Now both Dominic and Father Bosco have been named saints.

Saint Dominic Savio, patron saint of young people, help me to stay close to Jesus, too.

Saint Dominic lived from 1842–1857.

He was born in Italy.

We celebrate his feast day on March 9.

Saints Ann and Joachim

Joachim and Ann lived a long time ago. They were married to each other. They prayed that someone would come to save their Jewish people. God heard their prayers. He sent them a beautiful daughter. They named her Mary. She was loving and good. One day the Angel Gabriel told Mary that God wanted her to become the mother of Jesus, his Son. Mary said yes! She married Joseph, a gentle carpenter. Joachim and Ann became the grandparents of Jesus, our Savior.

Saint Ann and Saint Joachim, please help me to love Mary and Jesus as you did.

Saint Anne and Saint Joachim lived in the first century.

They were born in Palestine.

We celebrate their feast day on July 26.

Saint Paul Miki

When he was young, Paul went to a Catholic school. He learned to teach about Jesus. He wanted everyone to find the joy of being Christians. Many people listened to him. The emperor of Japan believed lies about Christians. He tried to send them all away. Paul and other Christians hid. They taught about Jesus anyway. Twenty-six brave Christians were captured and put to death. They loved Jesus with all their hearts. Paul Miki was one of them. In just one year, he would have become a priest.

Saint Paul Miki, please help me to follow Jesus' teachings the way you did.

Saint Paul lived from around 1562–1597.

He was born in Japan.

We celebrate his feast day on February 6.

Blessed Kateri Tekakwitha

Kateri's mother was a Christian Algonquin. Her father was a Mohawk chief. When Kateri was young, her mother died. Kateri lived with her aunt and uncle. When she was twenty, missionaries came to her village. She learned about Jesus and was baptized. Some people in the village were angry with Kateri. They didn't want her to be Christian. The missionaries helped her to escape to a Christian village. There she lived a happy life. Blessed Kateri is known as the Lily of the Mohawks.

Blessed Kateri, please teach me how to be faithful to Jesus as you were.

Blessed Kateri lived from 1656–1680.

She lived in what are now the United States and Canada.

We celebrate her feast on July 14 (U.S.A.) or April 17 (Canada).

Saint Alberto Hurtado Cruchaga

The poor children in Chile loved Father Alberto. They ran to him when his old green truck came down the street. Father always had a smile for each one. He built a large home for poor and homeless children. He called it Christ's House. He started schools and shelters, too. He helped people find jobs. Father Alberto believed all people should help each other. Pope Benedict XVI named him a saint in 2005.

Saint Alberto, help me to be cheerful, kind, and loving just like you.

Saint Alberto lived from 1901–1952.

He was born in Chile.

We celebrate his feast day on August 18.

Blessed Teresa of Calcutta

Mother Teresa worried about the many poor people in India. She knew Jesus wanted her to help those who were without hope. Thousands in Calcutta were sick and dying. Mother Teresa and the Missionaries of Charity started homes to care for them. Some got better. Others died peacefully. Soon the sisters started helping in other countries, too. They fed the hungry. They took care of the sick. Mother Teresa and her sisters wanted to weave a chain of love around the world.

Blessed Teresa, teach me to care about people who need help.

> Blessed Teresa lived from 1910–1997.
>
> She was born in Macedonia, formerly Albania.
>
> We celebrate her feast day on September 5.

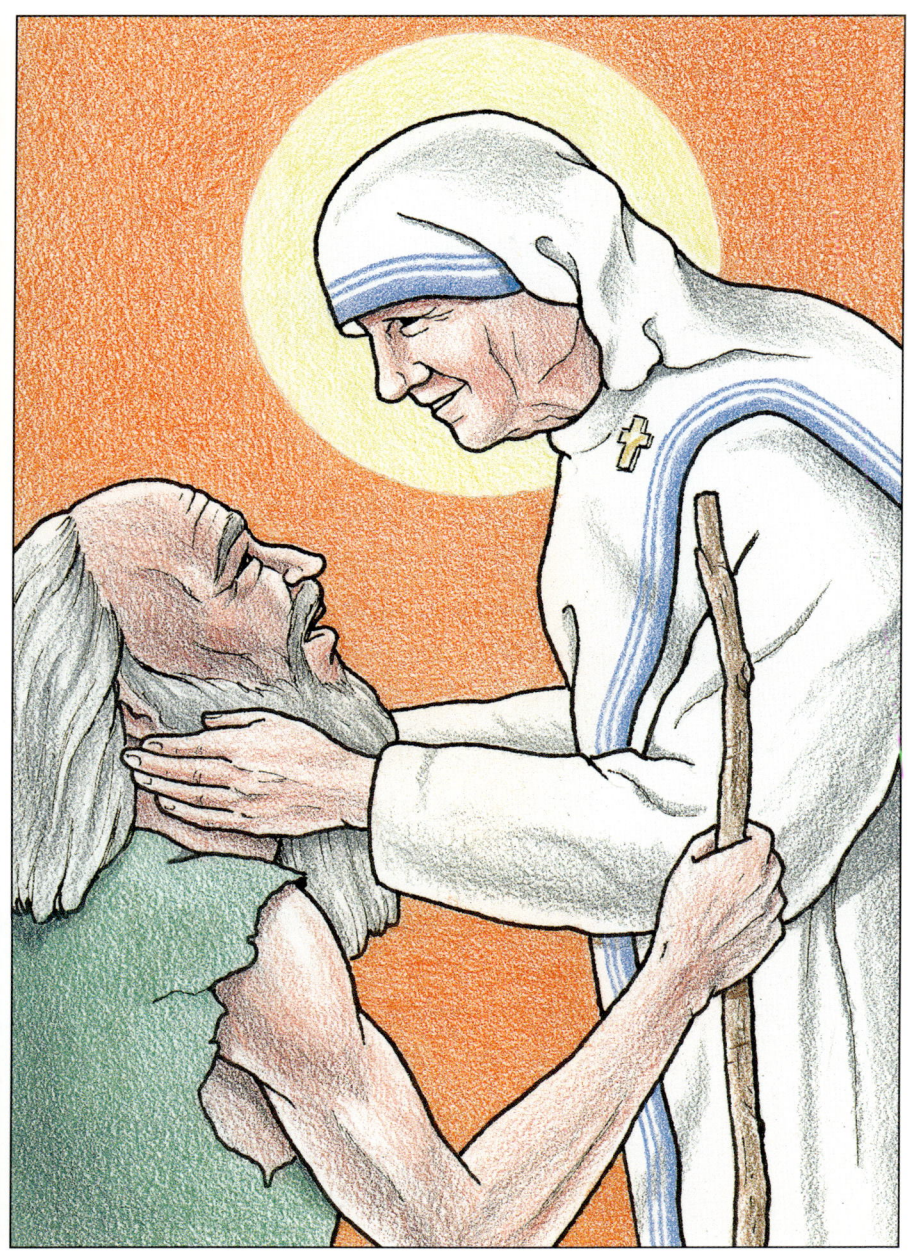

What Is a Blessed?

When a person has been named blessed, the pope has declared that he or she has lived a holy life and is now in heaven. Usually a miracle has taken place through prayers to the person. This is the next-to-last step on the road to being publicly declared a saint.

What Is a Saint?

When someone has been named a saint, the pope has declared that the holy person is to be honored by the whole Church. Usually a second miracle has been proven. This is the final step in being officially declared a saint.

What Is a Miracle?

A miracle is an amazing event that can't be explained by the usual laws of nature. The greatest miracle of all occurred when Jesus rose from the dead. When saints or blesseds perform miracles, God is working those miracles through them.